ABOUT VERVE POETRY FESTIVAL

Verve isn't your typical literary festival. Still only four years old, it has already made a huge mark on the national poetry scene, noted for its:
 Roof-shaking spoken word sets
 Readings and workshops by award-winning poets
 Boundary-pushing poetry/theatre performances
 Lively children's events
 and much, much more!
Most importantly, Verve is a festival for everyone to enjoy poetry together - where performance poets and page poets mingle and appreciate each others' art, where experimental poets swap numbers with childrens poets. Verve is for beginners and seasoned poetry afficiandos and everything in between. What ever kind of poet or poetry fan you are, no-one gets left out at Verve!

http://vervepoetryfestival.com
enquiries@vervepoetryfestival.com

Swapping The Present For A Future
The Verve Anthology of Beginnings

BIRMINGHAM

PUBLISHED BY VERVE POETRY PRESS
https://vervepoetrypress.com
mail@vervepoetrypress.com

All rights reserved
© 2022 all individual authors

The right of all individuals to be identified as author if this work has been asserted in accordance with section 77 of the Copyright, Designs and Patents Act 1988.

No part of this work may be reproduced, stored or transmitted in any form or by any means, graphic, electronic, recorded or mechanical, without the prior written permission of the publisher.

FIRST PUBLISHED FEB 2022

Printed and bound in the UK
by Imprint Digital, Exeter

ISBN: 978-1-913917-25-8

*To begin is to reimagine,
to rearrange,
to rejuvinate.
To begin is to lose and gain.
We are always beginning.*

CONTENTS

Foreword By The Verve Team

Introduction by Caroline Bird

And in the arrangement of salt - Tania Hersham	13
Good Luck To You In The World Of Teeth - Rushika Wick	15
Donor - Vanessa Lampert	16
Back Story - Helen Bowell	18
Cruelty - Luke Palmer	19
England says yes - Tom Sastry	21
I am one - James McDermott	22
Lara Croft is on fire - James Trevelyan	23
Primigravida - Estelle Price	25
The waiting room was purple - Maria Ferguson	28
A Neurologist Flips a Coin into a Well - Matt L.T. Smith	29
Barbecuing In The Snow - Christopher Horton	32
Knitting Nan-Nan - Kathryn Bevis	33
Eden the Robot Gardener - Ben Rhys Palmer	34
When I Marry a White Man - Helen Quah	36

Scarecrow's Parable - Prerana Kumar	38
Red Pepper - Ellie Jenkins	40
Caravaggio In Three Acts - Julian Bishop	42
In This Scene - Catherine Gander	45
Spectral Finish - Rachel Chong	47
Brain Surgery on Prime Time - Christopher M James	49
My Grandmother and the Coyote - Katie Hale	51
Silk - Olga Dermott-Bond	53
Sestina as green train no 3256 reflects on end of life - Annina Zheng-Hardy	54

Notes & Acknowledgements

FOREWORD

The theme of our poetry competition this year, after a year off in 2021 for obvious reasons, was *beginnings*. We wanted to hear how people felt about the prospect of making our first small steps out of the pandemic hiatus, fully knowing that while some would crave the return to some kind of normality, others would be all too aware that nothing can ever be the same again, that things have changed and the pause has either been a reset or a period of damage impossible to repair.

Our themes in these competitions always produce a wild and varied response, both in the terms of poetic content, form and style, which always pleases us greatly. And Caroline Bird, our judge this time, was faced with a bulging delivery of entries to dive into and emerge from with just three prize winners and a further twenty-one commended poems. The number of entries trebled on previous years, suggesting to us that perhaps one of the things that had been beginning during lockdown was a more productive engagement with and writing of poetry – one that matched the undeniable fact of the increased level of book purchasing that occurred. And for everyone embarking on a new attempt to write poetry, there were others, we know, who had returned to the fold after taking time away with a renewed purpose and a new vision for their craft.

This year at VERVE, the feeling on beginning again after our year off feels palpable. Beginning but not being the same, with our new hybrid festival, and our new focus on involving young poets, properly, as a central part of the festival and not just an afterthought. So we are thrilled to present you with this anthology of beginnings. Dive in and enjoy and let's all find our way forwards.

The Verve Team
Stuart, Lizzie, Kibriya

INTRODUCTION by Caroline Bird

It might seem like a crashingly obvious thing to say, but judging a poetry competition requires reading a lot of words. Words everywhere, until they're pooling in your coffee mug and rattling in your slippers. And you doubt yourself - acutely aware of the emotional and intellectual labour each poet has taken - desperate to stay focused, give everything a proper chance. You keep thinking 'What if I miss something? What if the perfect poem floats past me whilst I'm drowning in the alphabet soup of my own head?'

But then - BAM - the words disappear. Or rather, the words hatch. The words fizz against each other, chemically reacting. The words rise up from the page and fuse together like pixels to form images and you find yourself not reading but experiencing, and it doesn't matter if you're tired, or moody, or distracted, the poem snaps the fingers of a first line and - "shut up, it's starting" - a poem is on. It's happening.

It seems strange to talk about words disappearing from poems because, of course, words are all we have, they're our tools, ingredients, flesh, bones, the body of the thing. But something needs to occur in the placement of those words, the mixture and mystery, that animates the body into life. Anne Carson once said, in an interview, 'I'm trying to make people's minds move,' and, for me, that's what a good poem does: it tears through the membrane of the page that separates one mind from another, and jumps (tumbles, creeps, saunters) out into the world.

These poems all did that. They jumped into the world.

About the winners

1st Prize- Eden the Robot Gardener
Adrienne Rich once wrote 'the moment of change is the only poem' and that's what this poem does, it changes inside the chrysalid of itself. We watch as Eden (The Robot Gardener) develops, from obedience to decision to conscious thought. It's a very serious poem, disguised, as seriousness often is, in a playful conceit - but its world is almost real, near-future, fully imagined and imaginable; this is surrealism that hovers just a centimetre above realism, so close it grazes the earth. The ending, like all great endings, feels equally inevitable and unexpected.

2nd Prize- Cruelty
This poem embodies its subject: it squirms on the page and splits itself down the middle to reveal what Walt Whitman called 'the thin red jellies within you, or with me.' The language is totally alive, ruthless, thrillingly precise. And although it holds its words lightly, like grubs, the poem never once lets the reader wriggle free.

3rd Prize- When I Marry a White Man
This poem is like a plane flying through an epic novel, or a sped-up dream, it covers so much ground and, even though it's a longer piece, it feels as short as a sonnet because it positively aches with the unsaid. It's so taut you could floss your teeth with it. But then, when the plane of the poem finally lands, we have somehow seen a whole life - in fast-forwarded glimpses - and we're dizzy and reeling. The last line slaps us awake.

Caroline Bird
The Verve 2022 Competition Judge

Swapping The Present For A Future

And in the arrangment of salt
Tania Hershman

with pepper,
teapot, cup and saucer, water
bottle with its curl
of cucumber, glasses
drunk from, menu

And in the arrangement
of mother with daughter,
husband and wife, dog,
or cat with its curl
of tail, beds
slept in, a house

And in the arrangement
of salt with wife,
cat and daughter, saucer, husband
with no curl

And the table: reset

And the flowers refreshed,
salt and pepper filled

And the woman before
mother/wife

And the husband, tea
pot, cup and saucers

Salt the woman, pepper
her unchildren, curl
the unbecoming husband, refill
the dog, leave the water
bottle out, sit down
at the unwiped table, push
your cup, lick the menu clean. You can order
everything.

Good Luck To You In The World Of Teeth
Rushika Wick

Quiet in birth, astounded
swimming in smoke
before the police siren opera
kick in (the door)
your mother flounders in a
Mermaid Martini
each drink a sink
to keep afloat.
See how she watches
the slight movement
of your chrysalis eyelids, filigree veins
flushed with life,
Moon Opal in a locket.
Truth is, that there's no room for
gentle souls like her.
The papers are readied but
how many people nearly die
trying their best to love?

Donor
Vanessa Lampert

I guess your body must have always had
those extra special cells, tucked inside
your bones, long before their place
in someone else's story was announced.
Once those cells were yours and yours alone.
Watching your team smash it two-nil at home,
roasting a chicken with lemon,
walking the dog in the early morning,
when the sky above the park turns pink
and it's just for you. You weren't to know
someone in a lab coat, in a lab
was doing the maths, narrowing the odds,
solving a problem that wasn't yours.
Preparing to give your cells a starring role
in which they would appear as the answer.
You weren't to know that a woman
was waiting for your cells to be given
to her body, so they could bloom
like a dahlia in November,
flaring orange against the frost,
when summer had seemed lost forever.
Now you must live with the gratitude.
And didn't you say what you most feared
was a marching band and shiny
helium balloons saying THANK YOU?
Cheerleaders with red pompoms,
performing routines outside your house,
all of them chanting *thank you*. Didn't you say

that kind of THANK YOU would make you want
to ask for your stem cells back?
And now it's her turn. She gives you
a jade bead on a chain. You'll wear it
for the rest of your life. You call her your sister,
because you never had a sister until now

Back Story
Helen Bowell

So I made myself a seagull
dyed everything grey and white
glued sexless feathers to a Weetabix box
and circled the school carpark

bombing children with lip-shaped
sweets if I liked them
and smaller creatures' eggs
if I didn't

hovered by the gates studying
how girls in bunches became bananas
still green and hard
but not as hard as me

I was an unblinking seagull
always out of reach
I was the chip-stealer
the sky-klaxon

a squark so loud
nobody would want
to hurt me
couldn't if they tried

and I beat my wings
till the white vans and boys
in their bad uniforms simply
blew out to sea

Cruelty
Luke Palmer

You wonder how long this can go on
– Raymond Carver

Part of you meant it   the trowel born down
the pink flesh twiced   dancing
and you'd rather be honest than liked
so tell the full two minutes of this earthworm
turning in its axis   the coil of it jolted
by its wrecked snipped midriff as   further back
float the shrews you drowned in the canal
who bit down on their last breaths then burst
far off in dark water   up pops the rabbit
a mess of undergrowth by the time you'd done
its kinked neck uprooted   eyes bulbed
as you went again with the axe and then
     last week   the mauve-purple bloom
of a rats' nest mewling on your shovel
eight or nine blunt young at two days old
and useless   barely limbed and slow
through the parted warmth of the compost bin
these little rot-blossoms dragged themselves
as you wondered how to do it - a quick nick
with a blade to empty them like thumbs   or
a bucket   their dumbness shushed
in the end you couldn't stomach it
left them squeaking like saws trying to crawl
back to the warm earth   back to their mother
who won't come for them anyway
and she likely dugged with new litter so there
they lay alone   small marrow of small bones

leeching to subsoil   now the worm slows
you nudge it to a hole
press down the root ball of next year's crop

England says yes
Tom Sastry

You'll know someone like England
who knows what they don't like when they see it.
How they lean over the fence wanting to talk
about people's front gardens, young men
electric scooters, human rights.
How they love your bad news
a plan unravelling, a secret shame.
How they scan your body for signs of woe.
How you mock them and fear them
and are them, sometimes.

You didn't know that, today
England would be out on the street, your street
wearing bright colours and a friendly smile
head tipped back as if to catch the spray
voice fizzing like sorbet
around the delicious word *yes*.

They raise that voice higher *Yes! Yes! Yes!*
You smirk, sensing a joke to made
about Puritan sex. In that moment
you became England
and they are somewhere better
repeating their *yes*
like a prophet or, worse, a stranger
so foreign, so frightening, so vague.

.

I Am One
James McDermott

I am one when derek jarman dies of
aids   I am four when george michael is caught
engaging in lewd acts   I am five when
ellen degeneres comes out   I am
five when justin fashanu kills himself
I am six when gay age of consent is
reduced to sixteen   I am six when queer
as folk comes out   I am eight when brian
dowling wins big brother   I am nine when
gays are allowed to adopt   I am ten
when clause twenty eight is repealed   I am
ten when madonna and britney kiss   I
am eleven when civil partnerships
are passed   I am twelve when brokeback comes out
a gay hollywood love story   I am
fifteen when stephen gately dies   I am
fifteen when alexander mcqueen takes
his life   I am sixteen when stephen fry
shows clarkson what grindr is on top gear
I am sixteen when I spy curt in glee
my first time seeing gay boys in a school
on tv   I am sixteen when drag race
is first released   when rupaul tells me to
sissy that walk   to love myself   I am
seventeen when in eastenders   syed
comes out and is disowned by his mother
I am eighteen when born this way comes out
I am eighteen when michael causer is
killed due to homophobia   I am
nineteen when gay men can donate their blood

Lara Croft is on fire
James Trevelyan

after warm summer weeks playing   I run through a flame
and panic   I can't remember when we last saved
the game but I know hours have passed swapping
the controller on my bed   cracking hieroglyph puzzles
finally jumping that ledge   and so I felt again inside
that newly familiar kindling anger start to replay

and the certainty that you wouldn't come back to replay
these hours over if they were lost   all this as the flame
caught and burnt as it does   and lara writhed inside
a temple crypt   so I paused the game and saved
playstation is my domain   but you are already solving the puzzles
of your teens and changing interests   swapping

family for friends   and me three years younger swapping
innocence for awkwardness   still expecting to replay
the school breaks of our childhoods   the save icon puzzles
its way to completion   I unpause again and the flame
still burns over her   of course   and lara can't be saved
as her life bar drains and she lets out a groan from inside

reload from last save   except when it does she's inside
a temple cyrpt on fire   life bar draining fast   swapping
tomb raiding for doubling over and over because I'd saved
her in the act of dying   and though we watch this replay
in horror several times before trying to douse the flame
your energy falls fast too   this isn't one of the puzzles

you want to spend a summer on   your puzzles
are newly adult things with secret worlds you invite me inside
takes that I haven't words to reply to but make my cheeks flame
and my stomach blister about the life I'd soon be swapping
into growing up   and maybe just realising we'd never replay
this summer   or those past   that this may be the last you'd saved

some of your time for me   I load up that saved
game alone each day   trying to solve the seconds-long puzzle
of being on fire   run one way   no water   die   replay
but the oasis never comes and you are done being inside
on hot days while on the cusp of something greater   swapping
the present for a future   my sister a new burning flame

over I'd replay it so I might find you among friends and say   *I saved*
her   I put out the flame   drowning their laughter   there are more puzzles
inside this memory card   which   for your time and love   I am swapping

Primigravida
Estelle Price

Before

She was happy. Her body bubbled from its source -
a river unaffected by dams or diversions.

She had a scar on her temple since childhood -
it no longer mattered.

She thought of herself as 'possible'.

She ran like a dog let off the leash,
round the paths of Victoria Park, her legs humming.

She knew she had the right to say no
even when a prince unpinned her hair in the kitchen.

First Trimester

She was happy, or sad, each morning her belly heaved
as if trying to rid itself of the foetus.

She had a scar on her temple -
it belonged to a fairy story she couldn't remember.

She though of herself as possessed.

She ran along the Thames as if her arms were full
of boxes, husband latched to her side.

She knew her rights had changed but
she couldn't find the paragraph with the detail.

Second Trimester

She was blooming, they said. Her breats, two
one-eyed monsters in milky dialogue with her womb.

She had a scar on her temple but no one
not even her mother, paid it attention.

She thought of herself as an experiment.

She ran awkwardly like a clipped dog with three legs
who never looked in the mirror.

She knew that rights and what was 'right'
were two alternate stories, in a lifetime's collection.

Third Trimester

She was bursting. Her naked body a giant plum
its wrinkled stone demanding an exit.

She had a scar on her temple. She scratched it
to make it throb like it had before.

She thought of herself as context.

She ran, in her imagination, into the river and out
the other side without getting wet.

She knew she didn't want a caesarian but
on the day of the birth it became - necessary.

After

She is empty. Her body wants back the baby
cut out like a jewel from a wolf's belly.

She has a scar on her temple from her mother's
torment, when she was seven. A small hand grazes it.

She thinks of herself as riven.

She runs, after six weeks, east towards Hackney marshes,
husband left watching the crib.

She learns the knotted language of kith. Need pulses,
blends at her wrist, hers and her daughter's.

The waiting room was purple
Maria Ferguson

Purple walls, purple tables,
purple canvases of purple
fields and perfect purple skies.
The reclining bed was purple
and the curtain, and the chair
for my husband holding himself
where I would be if I wasn't
naked from the waist down
closing my eyes and wishing I had
a cupboard full of vitamins.
Lion stamped eggs. Some kind of
sparkling elderflower muck
to drink on Friday nights.
In the consultation room I stared
at the purple flowers in their purple
vase and imagined my insides;
an ocean, a cave, a storm.
Purple pebble washed up on the shore
as a nurse passed me the booklet.
A word starting with M and ending in E
- like mirage. Like mistake. Like mine.

A Neurologist Flips a Coin into a Well
Matt L.T Smith

on one side of the coin is a clear head of lesions,
on the other the point in the spine where man shed his prehensile tail,
that I would surmise, from experience, was likely hacked off
by some wayward immune system
that declared with drunken confidence:
This isn't supposed to be here.

I spend five years with a thermometer for an eye
watching heat linger like breathe on cold glass,
notice how the steam from a roast dinner
turns into a fog so thick my left eye can't make out my face
in the mirror.
The MRI shows no white matter lesions on the brain.
I still wait for the chime of metal hitting stone
to ring out, cut through the soft hum of living.

When dinner gets cold
the coin finally reaches the bottom of the well.
It doesn't make a sound.
My body becomes the site of a silent accident.
Friends place flowers between the ninth and tenth thoracic vertebrae
where my wayward immune system whispered:
This isn't supposed to be here?

Mum sits at the foot of my bed and gently pats my feet
the way she would when I was small and poorly.
I tell her *I can't feel it.*
I think something trite like:

I'm losing touch in a world without touch, smirk to myself
and remember the last time I hugged a friend in parting,
at arm's length, as she nervously laughed "I don't have it, I promise!"
before I stepped onto the tube, entered the tunnel
and alighted a year later birthed breach from the womb of an MRI,
numb.

I float down hospital corridors.
I float down streets these legs have known since they were small,
legs still in bed, street out the window,
street on a screen, another friend suggests we go on virtual walk on
    Street View.
Long before we knew each other we spent a lifetime in the same place
and she's curious to know where I live, so I show her roads
unfamiliar to her feet, ground which has become a stranger to mine.

My feet have become a stranger to me.
I float, a one-shot, a ghost.
I show her my front door.

In the end it doesn't really matter how the coin landed,
there was a head clear of lesions
and a spine with the tail hacked off
and the vertebrae marked up,
and this was always going to happen.

On the day I was diagnosed with Multiple Sclerosis
I found a care-package on my front doorstep from my friends
filled with things I love;
Terry's Chocolate Oranges, Ferrero Rocher,

a plush Tom Nook, my own furry little landlord,
and it takes me a moment to even question how they knew my address.

I showed her my front door and I knew
I am supposed to be here.

Barbecuing in the Snow
Christopher Horton

Since you ask, I like barbecuing in the snow
because I relish that juxtaposition of flame
and ice, as each flake falls stoically
onto the cooking grate, losing its shape

to become something else entirely.
I like the way the smoke fills this yard too
(this small yard, attached to our new home).
See how it bellows out across the below-minus-air,

the way it fills that precious space held here
with new senses and flavours before its journey.
Inside your belly, our little one, our third party, grows

impatient. Our little one is not averse to stuffed mushrooms
but prefers Quorn chipolatas. You're in the snug,
reading up on what you can eat at twenty-four weeks.

The heating plate could do with a deep-clean
but I've got this. The sausages will not catch
even though they are whistling, slightly. The steaks

will remain on the right side of well done, I assure you.
The smoke is scented by an aromatic mix
of garlic, fennel seed and chive. Really, I've got this.

I'm still out here, in the snow. I'm taking it all in.

Knitting Nan-Nan
Kathryn Bevis

I cast her on with double-pointers, Sheffield Steel.
First, I do her slippers in shabby, worsted wool,

alternate rows of knit and purl. Then up the tan
support stockings that always rib around her ankles.

Her shines are fiddly - their cabled veins require another
(same-gauge) needle, slipping stitches back-and-forth.

I pause for a mug of tea, a custard cream, before I tackle
the vast, loose landscaps of her hips, belly, thighs.

My needles click like tiny typewriters and she spools
from them - her Fair Isle of stretchmarks, her bingo wings.

I knit the screeching polyester dress she wore to clean
the step, knit her freckled hands, her wedding band, knit

the tumour nestling in her breast. When I reach the last stitch
of her blue-rinse shampoo and set, she casts herself off.

Now, she lies in my lap as I once did in hers: her neck's
soft crepe, that trace of B&H, the shrill acrylic of her voice.

Eden the Robot Gardener
Ben Rhys Palmer

He's programmed to follow instructions:
lay down the mulch, deadhead the begonias,
keep the cherubs around the fountain birdshit free.
But since he discovered his master and mistress
cold and stiff in their kitchen one morning
he's surprised himself by venturing off-piste,
devoting an hour to counting tadpoles, another to lifting
the stones around the pond to admire the oddballs
beneath: the woodlouse in its dusty suit of armour,
the millipede, divided into more segments
than the breakfast television his mistress would watch
as she sipped her oolong tea. Eden's calls
to the emergency services had gone unanswered,
so he used his detachable spade-arm to bury the humans
beneath their beloved weeping cherry. His mistress
had ordered him to get rid of the caterpillars
that were decimating the bougainvillae, but
he decided to let them pupate. He watched them
as they spun silk pads, hung from them like miniature bats,
and slowly shed their skins to reveal the chrysalids beneath.
With the hyper precision of his microscopic vision,
the crinkled sepia surface of each chrysalis seemed to Eden
like the strange terrain of some unexplored world.
Yesterday a butterfly hatched before it was ready.
Just ragged scraps for wings. It fell to the lawn,
scrabbled in frantic circles before a magpie
stalked over and snatched it up. All that industry,
thought Eden, that intricacy of conception,

only to emerge so calamitously wrong.
In his recharging chamber at night he thinks
of them in their chrysalids, bodies breaking down,
cells rearranging, no way of knowing
what will survive of their changing.

When I Marry A White Man
Helen Quah

I

A set of conjoined twins we were.
Bevelled heads.
The moonlight held our silhouette
on the pavement. When the plane
landed we clapped. I'd said we should
do the same before we took-off,
instead of laughing you passed
the luggage. I thought about
saying something of the dignity
of a woman's pain but we were
already in our cab cramping.
You were squeezing my hand
in your fist like lemon cake.
Oh! I think, this is how it feels
to be precious.

II

When we entered our hotel room
my husband put the reciever
on the table and kept his shoes on.
The room smelt burnt like carpet
the stale colours of old sitcomes.
Beneath the sink, there was a dying
mouse. The time along the closest sea
expired long before we arrived.

I hear the TV switch off. "Come to bed."
With his arm up behind
his head, I fuck my husband.
He hopes our daughter will inherit my good will.
My dainty feet and strong legs.

III

I'm made of stains and hiccups.
There are old honeymoon photos
sunk into the top shelf of our marriage
taken on the same bridge my father
took my mother to. Back then
I expected the re-enactment
to be stunning but my husband
was threatened by the dirt
of the place and the sweat
and sun cream poured
into his eyes like traffic.
I'm left with the image
of a dog in pain.

IV

The babies have learnt to hurt
like him. I sometimes think
they laugh at his jokes
more than mine.
When the house is quiet
and I've emptied all kindness
from its fact I'll touch a face
in the wet mirror. pour over
my worn slab half myself awake
more brutal than before.

Scarecrow's Parable
Prerana Kumar

I watch you make dirty habit, counting love on your fingers
before the night's cassava is smoked with haldi-jeera

veiling how I plough the paddy field as Accha's pyre
clusters its kernel. Amma fastens her husband's skull
to my temples, the last bedrock in my mourning face.
A body staggers with its inheritance, then ossifies to bear it.

From the window, she watches my limbs begin to stilt
in the slurry, banana leaves plating from each bone-socket.
She blanches her grief, her other children counting breadcrusts
dipped in oil as Accha's ashes sleet with the wind.

The second month, my brother places taro at my stake,
gap-toothed as he is faithful to the surviving family ritual.
Two baby feet, and ungodly with hunger, he hawks back
his bounty within the week, leaving the writhing skins behind.

I cannot stop the shadows that crop the gates by the sixth season.
Amma's back shudders against the front door, the deep pulse
as her eyes roll back to shine their whites. I stretch my tongue,
noose my sister's strands from their freshly oiled scalps.

I warden sixteen cycles for each of my years.
Amma dries rubber sheets on my arms,
says my siblings are schooling now.
She pares her finger and carves the alphabet
into my back, unhemming my grievance.

Black beetles scurry out the cavity, take flight off the collarbone,
line a Laksham Rekha outside the family homestead.

The paddy stalks ululate in my palatined view,
pressing lost rhythm to the wind.

Red Pepper
Ellie Jenkins

I'm 19, cat-sitting, standing in the kitchen
of a house owned by a woman, not the council.
Surrounded by pasta and rice removed from branded packets
and placed in jars with tags written in chalk:
not 'shells' but Conchiglie (con-kill-yeh),
not 'bows' but Farfalle (Far-fell-yeh),
and every spice from star anise to homegrown
herbs on the windowsill by the sink.

This is a white woman's pinterest wet dream:
rustic, cottagecore, beams on the ceiling,
Farmhouse, green-living, home crafts, country kitchen
and me, with my head in an American fridge-freezer,
in awe of the water dispenser, the slate-grey sleekness
of double doors flung open. I see:
Greek yoghurt, homemade samosas, and smoothies
with names like 'Green Machine'.

I am incongruous
to shelves in a kitchen and well-travelled fridge magnets,
to a rocking chair tucked in the corner with blankets,
to the red pepper, rolling around the bottom drawer
that I promise to replace when I smell its freshness,
losing to the pull of redness in my hand; it wobbles,
waiting to meet the solid oak chopping board
as I google how to cut it.

Here, there is a moment of promise: the blade of a knife slices
around the stem with amateur precision.
The blade manoeuvres the seeds, the watery-sweet flesh of the beast:
Google's recipes have no end -
"raw, roasted, fried,
stuffed, souped, sauced, spread"
but I have time to try them all,
and seeds wrapped up in kitchen roll,
tucked tightly in the back pocket of my jeans,
so I can place them in the windowsill at home.

Caravaggio In Three Acts
Julian Bishop

(with a nod to Billy Collins' Aristotle)

This is how it begins: a pair of peaches
only just fallen from the branch,
a paniere of reddening cherries.

Things are simple as Bacchus and a carafe.
Dawn of a new age of painting:
young Michaelangelo Merisi touching up

white horses with wings for Cesari.
This is the antipasto,
a first glimpse of the Eternal City,

morning sun glancing off a cupola.
Fame is a lizard's tongue flickering.
This is the priming of the canvas, animal glue

sinking into linen to emerge as a beautiful boy.
This is the opening, an Offertory prayer
murmured at the altar's cloth

in front of the Saviour's body.
Trumpet toccata, the instrumental ritornello,
a velvet curtain that ascends.

*

This is the middle, the apples scabbed
but still edible, worm gnawing at pith.
The horse is starting to buckle,

fruit bowls - already overloaded - waver
at the table's edge.
Abraham's hand stayed by an angel,

the opera meandering into aria.
Nothing is secure anymore.
This is the half-way chapter, murder contemplated

and committed, suspect on the run.
Layer sits on top of layer,
each applied thicker than the last.

This is the mezzogiorno, the sun at dazzling height,
full illumination of the body
while shade accumulates inside.

the priest intones *requiescant in pace*,
while fame takes the shape of Medusa,
beautiful but riddled with snakes.

*

And this is the end,
a cleansing of the chalice,
the weary priest who gestures dismissal

with a silent sign of the cross.
Here are the horses at the journey's end
eclipsed by a baby in the stable,

Salome with empty platter outstretched.
Fame mutates into many-tongued infamy.
This is where the widow wrings her hands

when Lazarus fails to rise.
In the wings, the majestic curtain is unhitched.
Canvas, long primed and painted,

requires more varnish to make it sing;
Dust and dirt stick to it, the glaze is cracked.
Carbon and Bone Black take eternity to set.

On the desolate beach at Porto Ercole,
the sunet is increasingly precarious.
The last ship to Rome long ago set sail.

In This Scene
Catherine Gander

I'm on my knees
    clumps of hair littered
        like unearthed flower stalks
on the bedroom carpet.

It's quasi-slapstick
(embarrassing, really)
how his foot swings to land again
on my backside
    collapsing me like a trestle table.

    PUTANA

Such passion.
My scalp tingles /
    his teeth foam with it
(It flecks my face; I close my eyes)

Minutes climb on top of each other
my mind is simultaneous
flashbulb calculus
    of all possible paths
    which will bring
    least harm?

The curtains are open
a streetlamp burns livid & no one sees
the effort we are putting in
rehearsing our ancient narrative.

TROIA

Out where the gods sit, a wind twists
the leaves, turning their twin faces
comic | tragic | comic | tragic

but everyone knows the stage is a lie
whatever is happening
is happening in the wings.

Day after night I've smiled
into footlights, absorbed their glare
and now I am nothing but bright air
empty as the mouths of masks.

Chekhov was right.
The gun was always there.
This is what you expected. Stand up.
      Exit.
He's still holding a bouquet
in his fist.

Spectral Finish
Rachel Chong

Today the paintwork of the 06.54 train popped
also the blushing ear tips of asparagus
pigeons and their burly chests beaming iridescence
wild bluebell heads (staring intently at their stems)
red onions with and without their paper skins

and in their radiance
surrounding objects celebrated
and/or grew envious for attention
mimicked their wavelenghts
so it glinted from the lids of yoghurt pots
refracted off pavement stones
onto the buckles of our shoes
and it was there ruminating
between lines of newspaper print
until the pupils of all the commuters
glowed like cherried moons

and the trains didn't mind
and the pigeons delighted
and the asparagus and the bluebells
and the red onions skinned and skinless
concentrated brighter
so others might join

a collective to project
not further just really to the interiors
where the rings of trees
and the crumb structure of cake
could see the world of indigo

so everyone would know
to look to the morning sun
behind its paper-screen mist
see it thread suspended droplets of water
and remember
that in the curvature of light
richard of york gave battle in vain

and continued bruising after death

Brain surgery on prime time
Christopher M James

It came knocking on her door.

In for a rough ride, she sits in a carwash,
water coming down like a stage-curtain,
hugging the shore of her handbag.

He drives now. From her passenger seat,
she waves, blows kisses to her kids
at the school gate before they vanish.

At last, she clasps a bed's side-rail
and evening sky flushes a warning red.
The surgeon hovers over a chart

as if readying a ping-pong serve.
Bodies do the talking, she holds his look
and her husband's packed hand.

The last scant meal delivered -
in the saving business too. Come dawn,
she hears voices in the unloading bay.

Whichever way the skull is sliced
she must talk through it all:
humanity's ten-thousand-year gift,

even counting gently up to ten.
Words must hold like stars
in the infinity of a cerebrum,

the surgeon lost in his telescope.
She senses the edges of the cosmos
are long plastic wraps. Later,

a hint of ceiling racing past,
thin air snaking over her skin,
a door's atomic blast.

Shapes lean in like trees among
branches of tubes. A split-second
question elbows through the foliage:

who's there?

My Grandmother and the Coyote
Katie Hale

It's true she first met him in the park,
pushing her neice in the coach-built pram,
him yapping some quip about babes.
He had breezed across the ocean on the weather,
all wisecracks and cheap
jackal laugh, his incisors lipped.

And it's true she first met him at a dance.
The girls were surging in their thin
print dresses, and in the band,
the Home Guard blew up a storm,
my grandparents face-to-face
shores of the Atlantic. They say coyotes
are supposed to mate for life.

And it's true she was a sensible girl,
but he was good-looking and American,

song dog with harmonics in his gait. He led her
down the narrow corridors of scales,
where every slick note was a door.

 And it's true they first met
on the threshold of the ROF, her bound
for the steps, for the brief
fumeless breathing of her break, him
loping down the byway with the troops. It's true
he called the dogged convoy to a stop,

his cry a steam train
shrieking on the tracks -

that he paused the whole goddam war
for their meeting. The road was hidden from view,
but it's true he was a harbinger of ending
and of birth, that his fur
furrowed grey and fulvous, and he bristled
at changes in the wind.

In their honeymoon London hotel, his breath
settled as meat. His eyes were lit and liquid yolks
and she believed she was part of his pack.

He curled and lengthened beside her on the mattress.
His body was the weight of a filled suitcase.

Silk
Olga Dermott-Bond

After 'Lady with a parasol, Madame Monet and her son' by Claude Monet

Lately, I have realised how
I need to piece tiny flecks
of colour together to make a word –

sentences spill and dissipate
like pollen across an open field,
wildflower-vowels skim elsewhere

instead of landing purple and red
at my feet. There is no such thing
as a straight line of sound anymore

bones are wind-caught, ribboned,
birdsong half-sung, thickening
rain-thrum a distant uncertainty –

when a child speaks to me, cloud
and shadow are crosslit by a careless
sun. Lately, I have realised how spoken

language is like a woman's twisting
body, spine and muscle caught
beneath layers of white rustling silk.

Sestina as green train no 3256 reflects on end of life

Amina Zheng-Hardy

last night you dreamt of your grave. the others were there.
    trees had begun to grow
        around under and through you: incidental
            monument of steel long defunct man—
                made machinery succumbing to godmade machination. it was
                    peaceful there but when you woke
to clamor: humans their convenience noodles their peeled orange
    you knew you would miss the way they can fall
        more easily in love with their own
            melancholy on hour 30 of leaving home
                staring out your windows beyond them
                    at the passing world

reappeared continuously. now you wish you could be kinder.
    but around you in your old age the world
moves more quickly. it has changed
    at the break of neck speed and so now you grow
more cruel with each year. can you remember
    the girl on her way home?
but there have been so many. the one who stood
    next to the man
no not that one a different one on a day you were packed so tightly there was no
    sleeping where for her with a fall
and a cut to the head that would
    scar she woke.

you cannot say you remember her.
    but later was there one who woke
with a start blanketless in phantom arms? on a day
    after on before the world
made many mothered girls—girls. you remember
    her pulling down her pants. fall—
ing over one of your shit smeared holes between clanging
    slabs of metal she grew
lessened. you wished your momentum could have been gentler
    on the man
too. the one who ran perpendicular
    from home.

and did he find that it is as hard to want to go
    as it is to want to live? you see them home.
the humans. but traveling only on this track there is so much you don't see.
    where they go where they woke
before you from where they came. you did not for example until it was too late
    see the man.
the sun trains its one mottled eye
    on the earth. the world
keeps its secrets from you. but now you know this. what is buried stays living
    all else passes away. you grow
weary sometimes watching children scatter from their playground on the tracks as you come
impermanent likewise not built to stand the test of time. fall—

owed. how it once thrilled you. the feeling of surfacing for air after a long tunnel.
terraced fields foggy mountains trees donning their fall
leaves. even the cities as they grew and greyed. the sky. in glimpses you saw them carry their
miraculousness. each building a home
to many that had once been housed in a womb birthed wiped off.
you wail an arrival and in the time it takes every willing heart on earth will beat grow
silent beat again. tonight like every night skyscrapers leak their blood skyward and in
your direction. bleach the night faces of the waiting as they woke.
they carry their bags on which they sat for days.
you feel ready to leave and leave this world
behind for the last time. there is a couple
that laugh as they find their hard seats. a woman a man

the way they can laugh. sometimes
    awe so strong you feel you must know this urge not just human
the desire to empty yourself then some days to stare and feel empty
    already less than nothing nightfall
that cannot be seen through
    the smog whirled
before it. the couple not sleeping hands moving beneath blankets
    a home
that can be made there
    in the space between. who woke
who first you did not see
    you see only the space and how it can grow.

in another life you see the man, his back is to you and he is faced toward home
in this life there is no fall, or if there is, he woke
the world will go on without you, in your next life from under the wheel trees will grow—

www.vervepoetrypress.com
@VervePoetryPres
mail@vervepoetrypress.com

THE POETS

Kathryn Bevis is a neurodivergent poet and poetry teacher, founder of The Writing School Online, and she was Hampshire Poet 2020-21. Her poems have appeared widely in magazines and journals, including *The London Magazine, Poetry Ireland Review, Mslexia, The Interpreter's House, Under the Radar,* and *iamb*. This year, a poem of hers came second York Poetry Prize and her manuscript *Mud and Spit* was highly commended in the Mslexia Pamphlet Competition. Kathryn designs and delivers Poetry for Wellbeing courses for adults in mental health settings, substance-misuse recovery settings and prisons. She's working towards her first collection.

Julian Bishop is a former television journalist living in North London. A former runner-up in the Ginkgo Prize, he's also been shortlisted for the Bridport Prize and longlisted in the National Poetry Competition. He won the 2021 Poets And Players Competition judged by Sean Hewitt with his poem *Sitting For Caravaggio*. He's also had poems in *Magma's Anthropocene issue, The Morning Star, XR's Rebel Talk, Finished Creatures magazine* and the first few issues of *The Alchemy Spoon*. He is one of four poets featured in a 2020 pamphlet called *Poems For The Planet*. His first collection is due out in early 2023 from Fly On The Wall Press.

Helen Bowell is a London-based poet and co-director of Dead [Women] Poets Society. She is a Ledbury Poetry Critic and an alumna of The Writing Squad, the London Library Emerging Writers Programme, London Writers Awards and the Roundhouse Poetry Collective. Helen won the 2020 Bronze Creative Future Writers Award and was commended in the 2021 Winchester Poetry Prize and the 2020 Mslexia Poetry Competition. Her poems have appeared in *bath magg, Poetry Birmingham, Magma, Ambit* and elsewhere. Her debut pamphlet *The Barman* was recently published by Bad Betty Press. She works at The Poetry Society.

Rachael Li Ming Chong is a writer, poet and teacher of Chinese Malaysian heritage, born and based in London. She is a graduate of the HarperCollins Author Academy and her writing has been published in various online platforms and anthologies, including *Poetry for Good*, Royal Society of Literature, *One Minute Monologues* (Atticus Books, 2021), *Where We Find ourselves* (Arachne Press, 2021), and *Words from the Brink* (Arachne Press, 2021).

Olga Dermott-Bond is originally from Northern Ireland. She studied English at the University of St Andrews and is an assistant head teacher at a secondary school in Warwickshire. She has always loved reading and writing poetry, and over the past five years has been dedicating more time to her writing. She has two daughters, and motherhood has shaped and influenced many aspects of her work. Memory, social and political history and female identity spark her interest as a writer and are prevalent themes in her work. Her first pamphlet *apple, fallen* is published by Against the Grain Press with the follow up, *A Sky Full of Strange Specemins*, published by Nine Pens Press.

Maria Ferguson is a writer and performer from Romford. She has been a resident artist for Roundhouse and Battersea Arts Centre and commissioned by Royal Academy of Art, Stylist and BBC Radio 1. Her show, *Essex Girl*, was shortlisted for Soho Theatre's Tony Craze Award and won Show of the Week at VAULT 2019. Her debut collection *Alright Girl?* was published by Burning Eye Books and highly commended at the Forwards in 2020.

Catherine Gander was born in Middlesex and now resides in Ireland, where she teaches at Maynooth University and runs a number of poetry initiatives, including the IRC-funded 'Diversifying Irish Poetry: Poetry Critics of Colour in Ireland' and the Maynooth Poetry and Poetics Series with Karl O'Hanlon. Her poetry, art, and essays have been widely published and anthologised. She was long listed for the Live Canon Prize, was runner-up for the Prole Poetry Laureate and has a series of poems forthcoming in Nine Pens Press's '9 Series'.

Born in Cumbria, **Katie Hale** is an internationally recognised poet and novelist. Her debut novel, *My Name is Monster* (Canongate, 2019), has been translated into multiple languages and was shortlisted for the Kitschies Golden Tentacle Award. Her second poetry pamphlet, *Assembly Instructions,* won the Munster Chapbook Prize. A MacDowell Fellow (2019), she won a Northern Writers' Award in 2021, and has been shortlisted for the Desperate Literature, Mslexia and Manchester Prizes. She has also written for theatre and immersive digital performance and has featured on national radio and television. She is currently working on her first full-length poetry collection.

Tania Hershman's poem, *And In the Arrangement of Salt*, will be included in her second poetry collection, *Still Life With Octopus* (Nine Arches Press, July 2022). *How High Did She Fly* was joint winner of Live Canon's 2019 Poetry Pamphlet Competition. Tania is also the author of a poetry collection, a poetry chapbook, three short story collections and a hybrid particle-physics-inspired book *and what if we were all allowed to disappear* and co-creator of the @OnThisDayShe Twitter account, co-author of the *On This Day She* book (John Blake, 2021), and has a PhD in creative writing inspired by particle physics.

Christopher Horton studied English and American Studies at University of Wales, Swansea, and subsequently taught in China before working as a Housing Officer and then as a Town Planner. His poems have appeared in P*oetry London, Poetry Wales, Ambit, Magma, The Wolf, Other Poetry, Dreamcatcher, Stand, Iota, Fuselit* and anthologies with Penned in the Margins, Broken Sleep Books and Days of Roses. He has been a prize-winner in the National Poetry Competition, the South Downs Poetry Festival Competition and the Bridport Prize. His debut pamphlet, *Perfect Timing*, is published by Tall-Lighthouse Press.

Christopher M James is a British/French poet, born in 1952. A former HR professional, he has lived and worked in France, Italy and Thailand, and currently resides near Paris. He has published three books in French, but since retirement has devoted himself to writing poetry in English. Recent poems have appeared in *Aesthetica, Orbis, London Grip, Ink, Sweat and Tears, Dream Catcher, Poetry Salzburg, French Literary Review, Best New British* and *Irish poets 2019-2021*, amongst others. He has also been widely anthologised and has won a number competition prizes, notably Sentinel, Yeovil, Stroud, Poets meet Politics, Wirral, Maria Edgeworth, Earlyworks.

Ellie Jenkins is a Bristol-based poet studying Creative Writing at Bath Spa University. Her work has previously been featured on *Ink, Sweat and Tears* and she has recently collaborated with Bookbarn International for National Poetry Day and Holburne Museum for their UpLate event series. Her poetry can also be found on Instagram @thepoetryhag.

Prerana Kumar is an Indian poet who has recently completed her MA in Creative Writing at UEA. She has recently been shortlisted for Nine Arches Press' Primers scheme and has been published in *Magma, Barren, Use Words First*, and *Ink Sweat & Tears*. She writes about how sense

sense of identity hinges on home, memory, desire, and the tenuousness of intergenerational inheritance.

Vanessa Lampert is an acupuncturist and poet from Oxfordshire. She has won the Café Writers prize, the Edward Thomas prize, the Sentinel prize and the Ver Poetry prize twice and come second in the Fish, Yeovil, Oxford Brookes and Kent & Sussex prizes. She was commended in the National Poetry Competition 2020. Vanessa's work has recently been published in *Magma, The Moth, The Oxford Times and Poetry Wales*. She co-edits *The Alchemy Spoon* and teaches children for Learn with Leaders in India. She has run workshops for Hive, Poetry School and Aldeburgh Poetry Festival. *On Long Loan* is published by Live Canon.

James McDermott's collection *Manatomy*, published by Burning Eye, was longlisted for Polari's First Book Prize 2021. Their pamphlet *Erased* is published by Polari Press. James's poems have been widely published in magazines including *Poetry Wales, Cardiff Review, York Review* and *14 Poems*. James was shortlisted for Outspoken's Prize for Poetry 2020 in the Performance category and Commended in The Winchester Poetry Prize 2020 and The York Prize 2021. James's plays published by Samuel French include *Rubber Ring* (Pleasance Islington/UK Tour) and *Time & Tide* (Park Theatre; Offie nominated for Best New Play 2020). James is also a writer on EastEnders.

Ben Rhys Palmer grew up in Cardiff, Wales. He lived in Barcelona for a number of years, teaching, acting and performing music, and now divides his time between Wales and Mexico. As well as writing poems, Ben works as a translator, songwriter and DJ. He has an MA in Creative Writing from Swansea University. His poetry has appeared in *The London Magazine; Forklift, Ohio; Poetry Wales; New Welsh Review; Wales Arts Review; The Caterpillar; Under the Radar; Interpreter's House* and *Neon*; and was commended in The Interpreter's House Poetry Competition and The Welshpool Poetry Competition.

Luke Palmer's second pamphlet of poems, *In all my books my father dies* (Red Ceilings Press) was released in 2021. Luke Kennard called it 'stark and beautiful....powerfully inventive' with an 'entrancing authorial voice'. His debut, *Spring in the Hospital* won the Prole Pamphlet contest in 2018. A graduate of the Bath Spa Creative Writing MA, Luke also writes novels for young adults. *Grow* (Firefly Press, 2021) was a Sunday Times Book of of the Year and was nominated for the 2022 Carnegie Medal. Luke runs the Bristol-based HOURS Writers' workshop and lives in Wiltshire with his partner and their two daughters.

Estelle Price lives in Cheshire but often goes west to the Llŷn Peninsula. She is learning Welsh. Estelle is the winner of the 2021 Welsh Poetry Competition and the 2018 Book of Kells Writing Competition. Her poetry has been placed/ listed in the National, Bridport, Welshpool, *London Magazine* and other competitions. Poems have left home for *Poetry Wales, Crannog, Marble Poetry, 14 Lines, Alchemy Spoon* and *the Stony Thursday Book*. She was also shortlisted for Primers 6. Before she knew she was a poet she was a lawyer, a classicist, a charity worker.

Helen Quah grew up in Romford, Essex. She is a poet and junior doctor working in North London. Engaged by the surreal, her writing explores the relationship of women in the modern world, mother and daughters, and the intersectionality of race in romantic relationships. She was shortlisted for the Aesthetica Creative Writing Award 2020 and her debut pamphlet is due to be published by Outspoken Press in 2022.

Tom Sastry's poems have appeared in *The Guardian* and *Poetry Review*. His collection *A Man's House Catches Fire* (Nine Arches 2019) was shortlisted for the Seamus Heaney Prize. His pamphlet *Complicity* was a Poetry School Book of the Year and a Poetry Book Society pamphlet choice. He is currently finalising a second collection due for publication in the first half of 2022.

Matt L T Smith is a Barbican Young Poets alumn. Matt was "handpicked by Joelle Taylor herself" to perform a set at the SLAMbassadors 2018 Showcase. His work has featured on BBC Radio 3 and Apples & Snakes Black Box series. Matt works with people with dementia on the project Finding the Words, developed by Anvil Arts, where he takes down the words of participants and turns them into found poetry. Matt holds a First Class Honours in BA Creative Writing with the Creative Writing Prize for Poetry and a Distinction in MA Creative & Critical Writing from the University of Winchester.

James Trevelyan grew up in the Midlands and now lives in South London. His poems have been published in various magazines and anthologies, and his debut pamphlet, *DISSOLVE to: L.A.* – poems from the perspectives of minor action movie characters – was published by the Emma Press.

Rushika Wick is a poet, doctor and Children's Rights advocate who is interested in how social structures and relationships impact the body. She has performed with the Cold Lips Magazine collective in London, Rough Night Press (Amsterdam) and Skylark (Norwich) communities. Her work has been published in literary magazines including *Ambit*, *Datableed* and *Tentacular* and within anthologies including *Fool-saint* (Tangerine Press), *Alter Egos* (Bad Betty Press) and *Smear* (Andrews McMeel). She published her first full collection with Verve Poetry Press in 2021.

Annina Zheng-Hardy is a writer living in London and @anneenzh. Her poetry and short fiction can be found in *Joyland* and *The Offing* among others.

ABOUT VERVE POETRY PRESS

Verve Poetry Press, now in its second year, is focussing intently on meeting a local need in Birmingham - a need for the vibrant poetry scene here in Brum to find a way to present itself to the poetry world via publication. Co-founded by Stuart Bartholomew and Amerah Saleh, it is publishing poets from all corners of the city - poets that represent the city's varied and energetic qualities and will communicate its many poetic stories.

We are also publishing more widely, providing a home for works that, for no fault of their own, are struggling to reach a readership. Our colourful pamphlet series, our spoken word show collections and debut collections that are packing a punch are available to order in all good bookshops and from our own site.

We are a prize-winning press, being named Most Innovative Indie Press at Saboteurs 2019 and winning the coveted Michael Marks Publishers' Awards for pamphlet publishing in the same year.

Like our sister festival, we strive to think about poetry in inclusive ways and embrace the multiplicity of approaches towards this glorious art. So watch this space. Verve Poetry Press means business.

vervepoetrypress.com